Self-Publishing
Success

A Simple 7 Step Formula for Writing and Publishing A Best Selling Book

BY

Jeff Leighton

Important Disclaimers

Table of Contents

Important Disclaimers 3

Author's Note 6

Introduction 7

Why You Should Write a Book 9

Step 1: Researching Competition 15

Step 2: Developing an Outline 18

Step 3: Writing Your Book 21

Step 4: Creating the Cover and Title..................................27

Step 5: Editing 31

Step 6: Formatting 35

Step 7: Marketing Your Book..38

Book-Writing Myths 56

Common Book-Writing Mistakes 63

Resources For Authors 69

Now It's Time to Publish Your Book 71

About The Author..73

Author's Note

This book contains additional resources that I use on a daily basis as an author and publisher. Since I could not physically include these in the book, they are all available to download for free on my website www.jeff-leighton.com. That includes helpful videos, recommended resources for self-publishing, additional training, and much more.

Introduction

Thank you for buying this guide. I have personally used these strategies to self-publish over 15 books and am proud to say I make a full-time income from my books as an author. You will learn exactly how to write, market, and publish your book on Amazon and other platforms and how to start making royalties and achieve celebrity status in your industry today.

While I publish non-fiction books, this guide contains helpful information for fiction authors as well.

The publishing game has changed completely. If you are an aspiring author, the days of submitting your manuscript to a big publisher and waiting years to hear back are over. In this day and age, you can publish on Amazon in one day if you want.

The floodgates have opened up. However, you

must follow the steps in this book to properly optimize and have long-term success with your book. Be sure to implement all of the strategies where possible. This is the beginning of your new life as a successful author and entrepreneur.

Why You Should Write a Book

There are countless reasons why you should write a book, from personal reasons to financial gain and many others. Everyone should write at least one book in their lifetime. I will tell you the quick story of how I published my first book and then get into all of the benefits of writing a book and how you can publish a book too.

I was working in real estate and building an investment company. I had always wanted to publish a book or create an information product to make a passive income and gain celebrity in my market place, but I just didn't know what to do.

At the time, the idea of off-market real estate was becoming very popular. Basically, off-market real estate referred to sellers who wanted to sell quickly but didn't want to use a real estate agent.

I had done a lot of these deals and worked with many of the top investors in the US and decided this would be my first book.

I came up with a basic outline and then wrote a lot of stories about my own experiences and the lessons I learned. It was a pretty rough book because I could not afford to get it edited or properly marketed.

However, because of the interesting real-life stories and all the value I offered in there, the book really connected with readers and still sells very well on Amazon. I now have over 15 books on Amazon and make a full-time income from my books alone. I got better and better with every book I published, and many of them have become Amazon bestsellers.

For starters, writing a book about a passion of yours or a fictional story can be a lot of fun and a great learning experience. You will brainstorm ideas, come up with an outline, and start creating your own masterpiece. There is nothing better than creating a product and publishing it.

Some people even use writing as therapy as it can

have a calming effect. I like to lock myself in my home office with a glass of whiskey and the Jimmy Buffett or Elton John Pandora station on. I could write for hours, and there is nothing better than creating something from scratch that is your own.

Another reason to write a book is the credibility and celebrity factor. Whatever your industry is, someone who has written a book becomes the expert and authority on the subject. Your clients will respect you more for having written a book. Not only that but if you market your book correctly, you will get noticed by the media as well.

This can lead to buzz around your book, which then leads to interviews, more publicity, and more clients. If you have a book, you can find the top podcasts for your industry and ask to be interviewed. I can guarantee that you will get a lot of positive responses and interview opportunities, which will only build your brand even more.

Amazon is the leading distributor for books these days and one of the top three search engines.

With your book on Amazon, more people will find you. No matter what industry you are in, you want to position yourself as the celebrity expert – not just the expert – and a book can help with this. A book is the best type of business card you can have.

Many non-fiction authors write books for the backend products and services that can be offered. While the money you make as an author is great because it is passive once you get your book out, there is a tremendous opportunity to earn an additional profit on the backend.

I would think of publishing to generate leads rather than make a fortune from an $8 book. Many non-fiction authors offer other products, training, courses, consulting, and public speaking.

If you can get enough people in your funnel buying your $5 or $10 book, there is always a certain percentage of people who will want more of what you have to offer.

As an author and entrepreneur, you should always have a low-priced ($10), medium-priced

($197-$497), and high-priced offer ($997-$9,997) around your products and services. A book is a great way to get people in the door as a lead generator.

Many non-fiction authors understand this concept and price their book very low to get as many people through the door as possible and take them through their sales funnel.

I would estimate anywhere from 3%-10% of people buying your book would buy another more expensive high-ticket product or service if you offered it. Take them through your funnel with different packages and priced services, and you will make the most out of each lead.

For example, I have this book which is under $10, but I also offer book publishing services on my website, at a higher price, as well as marketing services for aspiring authors. Some people just buy the book, while others will go all the way through and purchase all of my programs and services. You would be wise to offer the same, regardless of the industry or service you provide.

From building credibility with clients to gaining

publicity and making additional money with more products and services, there are numerous good reasons to write a book.

You will feel more accomplished than you do about almost anything you have ever done. Also, the best part of finishing your first book is starting on your second. You will be able to complete a second one in no time, and the process will be much easier the second time around.

STEP I

Researching Competition

When you are coming up with your book ideas, the most important thing you can do is research your competition. While you could just write a book about any subject in your niche, it would be much smarter to figure out what kind of books already sell a lot in your niche before you publish.

If you are not a celebrity and don't have a big following, then it would be a complete waste of time to spend years writing your memoirs, for example. Instead, model what types of books are currently selling well and are based on your interests and passion.

For example, if you don't have any ideas for your

book topic, go to your subject on Amazon and look at the top 100 bestselling books. If you don't know how to do that, then just Google "bestselling books real estate" or whatever your subject is, and the Amazon rankings should come up as one of the first results.

Take out a blank sheet of paper and start writing ideas for books based on the top-selling books. For example, I published numerous publications in the real estate investing niche since that was my specialty. Now, instead of publishing random books, I first studied the bestsellers list to come up with ideas.

If you do the same for whatever niche you are in, I can guarantee you that you will come up with ideas. When in doubt, just do a beginner's guide book to whichever subject you are thinking about writing. After you have 10-15 topics you could write about, you should spend an hour or two browsing all the good and bad reviews on Amazon for the similar books.

You want to know exactly what sells in your market and what types of things book buyers respond to. When I publish a book now, I know that it will be a bestseller, and not only that, but I know what the customers who buy this type of book are looking for, so I tailor it specifically to them.

Doing competitor's research before you publish a book is the most crucial part of publishing any book. As legendary marketer Russel Brunson says, you don't want to be a pioneer; you know who the pioneers are because they have arrows in their back.

He was referring to people who try something completely new and untested instead of finding something that is already successful and making it better with your own style.

Make sure you know the bestselling topics in your niche as well as the types of reviews people leave on similar books so that you can make yours better. Do not be the author who spends five years writing on some super niche topic only to find out that no one wants to buy that type of book.

Developing an Outline

Creating an outline for your book is one of the easiest things to implement and one of my favorite parts of writing a new book. You need to realize that it is challenging to write a book without an outline.

Not only that, but your book will come out disorganized if you don't use an outline. Having a well-prepared outline will make your writing process a breeze.

Once you decide on your subject, you should look at the top 10 selling books of a similar subject in your current niche. You can click on their preview link in Amazon to see their table of contents. For each book, you should write down the table of contents to get an idea of how your book should be structured.

After you have gone through at least 10 similar books, you can choose the 10 best chapter ideas and then use those as the general framework for your book.

Under each chapter, you should also include three to five bullet points of what you are going to cover in each chapter. I would spend an hour or two doing this and then come back to the outline a day or two later.

Repeat the same process by looking through other similar books for good ideas for chapters and subpoints to include in each section.

To gain additional ideas for your chapter outlines, you can do research online to add to the outline. Between these two strategies, you should easily have a framework for an outline. Do not even think about writing your book until you have a solid outline. This will make your writing process fast and easy.

You should now have a general framework for your book and be able to get the writing done easily without a headache. I would suggest including 10 chapters or sections in your book, but you can always do more or fewer, depending on your topic.

Make sure to include stories as well in each section. People love hearing stories as they can relate more to a story than a general type of tip or lesson.

STEP 3

———◆———◆———

Writing Your Book

Even though I don't have a formal background in writing, I can offer you tips from having published numerous books and making a full-time income from royalties as an author. The way I came up with these ideas is by learning from some of the top writers and marketers in the world, like Stephen King, John Carlton, Eben Pagan, and others.

But most importantly, I learned how to write from being in the front-line trenches, by writing every day, and eventually making a full-time income from my writing by finding out what works and what doesn't.

Once you have your general outline completed, you should start writing. Everyone has their own preference, but I have found that my most productive time is in the morning. I like to write for two or three hours bright and early in the morning when I am most focused. If you are more of a night owl, then that works too.

However, generally speaking, I would avoid writing around 2:30 p.m. That is when people tend to be tired. I know that I am not very creative during that time. Around 2:30 p.m. is when you should either be taking a nap or doing busy work that does not require a lot of thinking.

For the first round of writing, do not focus on editing – just get it on paper. In the editing process, you will go through a couple of rounds of edits, but for now, you just want the main draft done, based on your outline.

The next tip is one that I learned from multi-millionaire entrepreneur Eben Pagan. I find it very helpful to write or work in one-hour chunks.

Block out all distractions and set your timer for one hour. One focused hour is often better than other people's three or four hours of semi-distracted work.

After an hour, take a short break where maybe you get breakfast, do some stretching, work out, take a shower, or go for a quick walk. Then come back and do another one-hour power session of writing.

This is how I tend to work, and I have discovered it makes me super productive. You would be amazed at how much you can accomplish over the course of several days, weeks, or months with one-hour blocks of focused writing.

Another writing tip, which I learned from John Carlton, is to write as if you are talking to someone at a bar. Unless you are writing some type of medical journal, it is a lot easier to connect with someone if you write as if they are right there. You should not try to sound overly formal as if you are submitting a paper to a university professor.

Something that goes hand in hand with this idea is to include stories in all of your writing. If you don't learn anything else from this book, learn that stories are one of the best ways to communicate.

Try to include as many real-life stories from your own personal experience or from other people's experience that you can think of. This will make your communication easily understandable and more interesting.

People love stories, and I try to include them in as much of my writing as possible. In fact, after I write a draft of anything I publish, I go through each section and try to add in as many relevant stories as I can from my own personal experiences.

In fact, my first book that I published called Off Market Real Estate Secrets was not the most well written book. However, it was jam packed with tons of interesting stories from the real estate investing world and I still make a great passive income off of it to this day.

Lastly, do not think that your book has to be the same length as *War and Peace* or anything like that. In fact, for your first book, 10,000 words is perfectly fine. If you have an outline, this can be done in a week or a month.

There are many books on Amazon that have just 5,000 words, although I would recommend doing a minimum of 10,000 words. If you are feeling ambitious, then go for 20,000. If you can offer a ton of value in 10,000 words, then there is no reason to force yourself to write 50,000 words.

One reason why my readers like my books are that they are straight to the point and offer a ton of value. I decided to make my books short and to the point because I have read real estate books in the past that took me weeks and months to get through.

After reading them, I just asked myself, why? The author could have easily gotten their point across in one-tenth of the time. I could write 50,000 words and insert lots of fluff and unnecessary boring chapters if I wanted to but I see no reason to.

Instead, I cut straight to the chase and offer valuable information without having to read for 10 hours. In fact, most of my books can be read in one hour. I was tired of reading real estate and other publications that dragged on and on with regurgitated academic theories. Instead, my books are action-packed guides that get you the info you need quickly.

So there you have it. Basic tips for writing your book, but valuable nonetheless. Let's recap the strategies. Finish your outline and start writing – do not worry about editing for now.

Write in one-hour power blocks where you are completely focused and then take a short 10- to 15-minute break to refresh before sitting down again for another hour. It's amazing how much you can accomplish during a couple of these power sessions.

Next, be sure to write as if you are talking to someone at a bar and include stories as much as possible. You do not want to sound too academic or stifled.

And then lastly, do not think that your book has to be a 500-page textbook. For your first publication, you do not have to be perfect. 10,000 words is an excellent number for starters, and some authors do even less than that. The idea is to get it done and published, and then you can always improve on that book or the next one.

———■◆■———

Creating the Cover and Title

Your cover and title are the most important parts of your book. As people will judge your book by its cover, you need to spend some time making sure it stands out. There are literally millions of books out there, so your book has to be fully optimized.

When deciding on a cover, you should not try to create it yourself unless you come from a graphic design background. This is what I would recommend: spend an hour or two browsing all the covers out there, from bestselling books in your niche as well as other niches.

Try to find three to five covers that are eye-catching and that you really like. Then you outsource them to a graphic designer.

There are many places to do this, although I would recommend either Fiverr.com, Upwork, 99 Designs, or Reedsy. Fiverr.com is excellent if you are on a tight budget because for as little as $5 you can have a designer create a book cover for you. Upwork is great because you can choose from thousands of designers and there is a little bit more personalization than on fiverr.com.

For as little as $50 you can usually find a qualified book cover artist who will give you an amazing cover. 99 Designs and Reedsy are probably the best options if you are not on a tight budget. Some of the top designers on those sites have created the covers for *NY Times* bestselling authors and celebrities.

Your title goes hand in hand with your cover, and it is something you will also need to spend some time thinking about. The best title ideas come by doing a combination of two things.

First off, get a blank sheet of paper or Word

document and start copying and pasting the bestselling book titles of current books in your niche and others. This will start to give you some general ideas as to what type of titles sell.

Then you should start combining different titles and adding your own personal ideas. I would recommend coming up with at least three to five title ideas and then asking a couple of friends and family members which title is best.

You can also run a test on PickFu.com, where people can vote on their favorite title, and you can get feedback quickly. After going through this process, your title will be supremely optimized to sell and will have already been tested as a winner.

Overall, you need to really make sure your cover and title stand out from the crowd. By looking at bestselling books and titles and then using your own ideas, you should be able to have an optimized book ready to sell.

You should always try to test any idea as well before you submit it. PickFu.com is great to survey people on which title or cover they like best and you can also just ask a few friends or family members. Most authors do not spend much time on their cover and title when, in reality, they should spend the majority of their time on these two items.

STEP 5

Editing

Getting your book professionally edited is key to having a book that will sell and give you credibility. And it's not just a quick edit as if you are turning in a book report. If you are publishing a book for sale, this could instantly boost your career and earnings, so you need to make sure you take it through an editing process.

Fortunately, it is easy and straightforward to do. In this section, I will take you through my editing process.

Step one in the editing process is to write your entire book without stopping every few minutes to think about editing. You want to flush all the ideas out first before you start making changes.

After I write a book, I like to give it a couple days or a week and then come back to take a second look at it once I'm refreshed. Within that week off, I might have come up with new ideas or insights I want to add.

Moreover, this short break allows me to look at the writing with a fresh set of eyes. I will go through the entire manuscript and highlight weak parts of the writing or parts that clearly need to be fixed. Then I go into each part and re-write it as needed so that it is a solid manuscript that is almost ready to print.

After reviewing it a final time, fixing any other errors and tightening the book up, I send it to a professional writer and editor to edit. I try to have the book completely done and already edited a few times before I send it over to my editor.

Step two is critical because a lot of authors either skip this part or send their book to a friend. When it comes to publishing a book, you need all aspects of your publication to be in the top 1%

because all the different factors will add up. If you skip this part or have a buddy edit your book for you, there will almost certainly still be errors in your writing.

I use professional writers to edit my book because they are better writers than me. They can see things and re-work things that I would not even think of. Having a qualified writer help you with your work is a no-brainer. Top notch editing is more affordable than you would think and will significantly boost your credibility as an author.

There are a couple of services I recommend, including Postscripting, Reedsy, and Scribendi, where you can get instant quotes and read the biographies of the writers who will be editing your work.

The next step is key. Once I get the fully edited manuscript back, I go through the entire guide and read it aloud. This is important because even a skilled editor is not perfect. I can guarantee you there will still be smaller things here and there that need optimization. Once you read it aloud and fix any small things, then you almost will be ready to publish from an editing standpoint.

The last editing step I go through is to take my manuscript through Grammarly or other online automated editing service. This will give your book the final touches and there will be smaller edits that Grammarly will catch.

You are now ready to publish your book from an editing standpoint. However you still need to format the book, which I will discuss in the next section. That part of the publishing process can easily be outsourced.

Whatever you do, do not skimp on editing. There are countless self-published books that were obviously not edited properly. Those books come across as amateurish. As a result, they get bad reviews and don't sell many copies.

Formatting

Formatting is the most overlooked part of publishing on Amazon. What most authors don't realize is that even if you are on a tight budget you can still pay to have your book's interior look exactly like a *NY Times* bestselling book. Just browse through different books on Amazon by clicking on the preview, and you'll see what I mean.

Many authors and publishers are lazy when it comes to formatting, which means you have a massive advantage if you get your book correctly formatted.

The formatting is how your text will appear in the

book. You do not want your writing to look like a book report from 7th grade, double-spaced with a Courier 12 font. Instead, you should model the bestselling books.

I have a professional book formatter that I work with for a reasonable price. I send him the text and a couple of screenshots of what I want the formatting to look like. Of course, I only send him screenshots of the interiors of top-selling books that I like.

Then, within a few days, my full text is formatted perfectly so that it looks like it came from a billion-dollar publishing company. Now, Amazon has a helpful guide on how to format a book yourself. I did this for my first book, and it came out pretty well.

That being said, this is something you should outsource since there are experts that can get it done quickly and affordably on sites like Upwork and Reedsy.

You need a professional because the formatting for a paperback version and a Kindle version are different and the spacing can get messed up quickly if you try to do it yourself.

It is very easy to put in an extra space or indent which can skew the entire layout of your book. That is why I recommend paying an expert. Once you get the book back from the formatter, you will go through and review it. If it looks good, then you are ready to publish.

Overall, you would be shocked by how many authors ignore the two basic steps of editing and formatting. If you want to be a successful author and make a full-time income, or at least an extra couple of thousand dollars per month, then you have to take care of these two steps.

They are not that expensive, and I can guarantee you that they will make your book better. As the legendary marketer Frank Kern said, "Perception is reality." You want your book to be amazing, but you also want it to look and feel amazing. By getting it edited and formatted correctly, you will be in the top one percent of authors.

STEP 7

Marketing Your Book

Marketing your book correctly creates the difference between your book selling or just taking up space on Amazon. If you want to make a consistent passive income and build your brand, then you need to not only write an amazing book but also use the proven marketing strategies below. It does matter how good of a writer you are, if your book is not properly optimized then your sales will suffer.

There are probably hundreds of marketing strategies for books out there, but I have chosen the 10 essential strategies that I use and that are REQUIRED if you want to sell your book. All of these tactics are straightforward and easy to implement, yet 99% of authors do not do apply all of them. Most authors will do maybe one or two of these, but certainly not all 10.

The shocking thing is, many bestselling books are literally leaving millions of dollars on the table because they don't have the simple things that we will go over in this section. I have mentioned some of them earlier in this book, but I want to reinforce the fundamentals to position your book to sell as much as possible.

I believe in stacking up as many advantages as possible in your favor as an author, so ignore these tactics at your own peril.

Marketing Strategy #1

The fundamentals of marketing your book include getting a professional cover and a catchy title. These items should be outsourced to experts who do this stuff for a living. Fortunately, these services are all relatively affordable.

For your cover, you should hire someone on Upwork, 99 Designs, or Reedsy. Give them three or four screenshots of bestselling book covers you like and tell them to make it look like that. They should give you a couple of renderings and then you can choose a final design and go from there.

For your catchy title, you should make a list of bestselling titles in your genre or others that stand out. Then mix and match different parts of those titles and create your own catchy title based on bestselling ones.

Once you come up with three or four title ideas, you should do a survey on social media, Pickfu, or just ask a few friends what they think and then go with the most popular one.

Next, make sure you use a talented writer to edit your book so that it comes across in the best possible way. There are plenty of amazing writers that can edit your text on services such as PostScripting, Scribendi, Reedsy, and others. You can get instant quotes for these services on their websites.

There are many authors who will never be discovered because they don't take the time to properly research and create a cover and title.

Marketing Strategy #2

One of the easiest and most overlooked ways to dramatically increase your book sales is to have the book available in 3 different formats: Kindle, paperback, and audiobook format. Nine out 10 of authors skip this part.

In some cases, even bestselling books published by big publishing companies leave millions of dollars on the table because they're not available in several formats.

You need to take up as much internet real estate – so to speak – as possible. If you offer your book on multiple channels, you will see an increase in sales. It is very affordable to format your paperback on Upwork or Reedsy, so you would be crazy to ignore this part. Many people still prefer paperbacks.

The audiobook option takes a little bit more money and effort, which means that hardly any authors go this route. That leaves a big opportunity for you. They don't realize the audiobook business is booming and they are missing out on vast amounts of money by not producing an audiobook.

There are a couple of ways to get an audiobook produced. You can buy audio-recording equipment on Amazon and record it yourself and then hire an audio tech on Upwork for $100 to take out noises and make it sound professional once you're done.

You can also hire a narrator for either a royalty split, where you don't have to pay them anything up front, or for a flat hourly rate. For a good narrator, the hourly rate is usually in the range of $150-450. A good rule of thumb is that every 10,000 words is 1 hour.

I would recommend paying the hourly rate of an experienced narrator. Your book will come out sounding great, and you won't be tied to making royalty payments to someone for eternity.

There are also companies like Lulu, IngramSpark, and others that will also inexpensively create a hardcover for your book. Technically, one book could provide you with four digital products, since four different formats give you four different passive income streams.

Marketing Strategy #3

Next on the list of required marketing strategies is SEO or search engine optimization. You need to be strategic about this so that, when people type in a book subject they are looking for, such as "how to invest in real estate" or whatever your topic is, your book shows up.

When you submit your book on your Amazon KDP account, there is an option to choose seven different keywords for your book. There are a couple of ways of finding the most profitable keywords.

The first way is to use a paid keyword search tool such as KDP Rocket. This service will tell you exactly how much that keyword is worth per month in income and which keywords to use. There are similar services available although I would highly recommend checking out KDP Rocket. It will save you time, and this is what all the pros use.

The free way of finding keywords is this. First, you need to get a blank sheet of paper or Word doc and start compiling a list. Log out of your Amazon account and open a new browser window.

Go to Amazon to do some keyword research. Once you have Amazon opened in a new browser window so that it does not remember your settings, you can start typing in the first word or two of your subject and compiling a list.

Amazon will autofill the most popular keywords, which are the ones people search for the most. They don't tell you exactly how many people are searching – like KDP Rocket or Adwords does – but you can still get a good idea.

Look at the bestselling books in your own niche to get more ideas. Once you have a list, choose the most important seven keywords and put them in each box.

Next, you can add up to five keywords per box with just a space in between each one. Almost nobody does this. So add the next five most important keywords into the first box, second box, third box, and so on.

Keep in mind, Amazon does not care how often you repeat a keyword the way Google does. So if your book is about real estate investing, you do not want to write "real estate investing," "real estate investing tips," "real estate investing strategies." Instead, you would want to put in real estate investing tips, strategies, ideas, and not just repeat a variation of real estate investing 100 times.

This one strategy alone should catapult your book up the rankings. You can also include keywords in your book description and title, but be sure not to make your title look too spammy with keywords.

Marketing Strategy #4

Having good reviews for your book also makes a massive difference in sales. Excellent reviews have a direct correlation to getting more sales, especially if you have several, not just one or two.

Before I get into advice on a couple of ways to get reviews, I want to warn you to never pay for a review. Amazon is very good at sniffing out any artificial reviews – or anything else, for that matter, that might negatively affect the customer. They might not catch it today or tomorrow, but I guarantee that they will catch you and could even permanently ban your book account.

The first strategy that works is to ask for a review at the end of your book. You can look at any top-selling Kindle book to see what I mean, but any author that has reached bestselling status has a simple and kind request to leave a helpful review at the back of their book.

Not everyone will leave a review. In fact, most people won't, but if you get 20 or 30 purchases, you should be able to at least get a review or two from there.

The next strategy is to ask for reviews from your email list when you first publish your book. Your email list could also be your social media; the point is to get several reviews so that other people feel more comfortable leaving reviews.

Nobody wants to be the first person to review a book, so having a couple of reviews from people you know should help to get things started.

If you have a series of books, be careful not to have your friend or family member just leave a string of five-star reviews. Like I said, Amazon is very good at removing anything artificial.

While you can ask friends, family members, and

associates for reviews, they have to purchase the book. Keep in mind that reviews cannot be obtained through a free Amazon promotion.

Lastly, price your book at 99 cents when you first release it to encourage more people to purchase it and leave reviews. Once you gain traction with the book and start getting more reviews, it is straightforward to increase the price to whatever you see fit.

Marketing Strategy #5

The next marketing strategy is to write a series of books. Once you have published your first book, you should congratulate yourself, go out for a nice dinner or a vacation, and then immediately start on your next book. It was not until I had about three books that I started making a good income on Amazon.

You will find the process of writing a second or third book 10 times easier than writing your first one. For example, if your passion is dog training and you wrote a book about *Dog Training Basics,* then your next book could be *Advanced Dog Training Techniques* or *How to Train Your*

Rottweiler or Chihuahua, or any number of dog training subjects. There are probably literally hundreds.

The point with having a series of books is that you can cross-promote each book and start to build your brand. When someone goes to your Amazon author page, they will see several books instead of just one.

Marketing Strategy #6

The next marketing strategy when doing a series of books is to try and build an email list. At the end of your book, you should ask people to submit their email so that you can stay in touch with them about any new books, additional products, services, and updates.

The idea is that you are building your brand and your tribe, so to speak. This will help you to build a list of customers who are interested in any future books you publish as well as any other products and services.

The best marketers use their books as lead magnets to offer higher-priced and more involved products and services. You should see your books as a funnel, and at the end of the funnel, there might be additional books, a course, consulting, public speaking, a mastermind group, and anything else you can think of.

This is where the real money is made, on the backend of things. One of the biggest mistakes I hear from a lot of authors and entrepreneurs is that they didn't build their email list early enough. Don't make this same mistake!

Marketing Strategy #7

Next, your book should have a fantastic book description on Amazon. If you do all of the things listed in this section, but you write an incomplete or boring description of your book, you will be missing out on a ton of sales.

The best tip I can give on writing a description is to look at the Amazon Author rank and find Authors in your niche who have great book descriptions.

For example, I am in the business niche, and some of the bestselling authors in my niche include S.J. Scott, Hal Elrod, and numerous others. You can follow the same format that they have in their book descriptions instead of just winging it. There are three things to keep in mind when creating a book description.

For starters, you should utilize HTML formatting when writing a description so that your headline and text stand out. All of the top authors utilize a big bold headline on their descriptions, and you should do the same. There are free numerous text to HTML conversion sites online that you can use to get this done easily.

Next, you should insert some of the keywords into your book description. This will help your book to rank higher on Amazon, and hardly anyone actually does this. Don't be spammy with your keywords and you should easily be able to add 5-10 keywords with a good description.

Lastly, too many authors have a book description of a few sentences. Your book description should be at least 250-500 words and take up a good amount of the space provided. And when in doubt just model the top authors' descriptions.

Marketing Strategy #8

The idea with publishing a book or any type of

content is to have it reach as many places as possible, in as many formats as possible. While Amazon dominates the book market – I've heard estimates of 60-80% of the market – there are other retailers out there that will sell your book as well.

Some of these include Apple iBooks, Kobo, Barnes and Noble, and hundreds of other smaller book distributors. There are a couple of ways of getting your book onto all of the platforms available.

The first way is you can upload your book or pay a virtual assistant to upload your book in all its different formats to each of these various sites. Each company will have slightly different formats so in my opinion, this can be a little tedious.

Fortunately, there are numerous publishing aggregator and distribution companies that will do all this for you. It will save you hours of formatting and uploading to all the sites.

Publish Drive is one of the companies out there that I recommend for this type of service. Even the big publishing companies ignore this strategy, giving you yet another opportunity to sell more than some of the big-name publishing companies out there.

Marketing Strategy #9

Another strategy for selling your books is to get them translated. Amazon is a vast marketplace, and you will be missing out on sales internationally if you don't do this. There are numerous languages that you can get a translation to. Just make sure you don't use Google Translate or a computer translator.

You need an actual person with good reviews to translate your book and then have someone else review it just to make sure. By using this strategy, you can create 20 or 30 different digital products from one book.

Let's say you wrote a book about *How to Adopt a Dog*. You can have that book in four different formats – Kindle, paperback, hardcover, audio version – and then you can get it translated into different languages.

If you had a series of books around your subject, you could theoretically have hundreds of digital products all making a monthly income stream for you, and you could build a worldwide brand instead of just the English-speaking countries.

Since it can be more expensive to translate a book, I would recommend starting with only one language like Spanish, seeing how effective it is, and then adding on additional languages.

Marketing Strategy #10

I have kept the best marketing strategy for last. If you are writing a book to make a full-time income as an author, then you need to publish a book based on what other books are currently selling in your niche. For example, unless you are a celebrity, nobody wants to read your memoirs that have spent years working on.

Instead, get ideas of what the bestselling book topics are and then reverse engineer and craft your book idea based on what is currently selling. You should look at topics of books that are in the top 100,000 of Amazon, which usually means they sell at least a copy or two every day.

Look at the Amazon product description of the book to see its current ranking, which gets updated hourly. If you write a book without doing any research on what sells on Amazon, then your book will most likely fail.

That is why, before I publish any book, I make sure there is a hot market for the topic I am writing about. I usually don't want to be the only book in my niche, in fact I prefer writing on topics that have tons of competition since I know it's a hot market.

By implementing these strategies, you will be in the top 1% of authors out there. It is incredible to me how the vast majority of authors and publishers don't even use some simple marketing strategies that could position their book significantly better.

I'm not even talking about self-publishers; I'm talking about big publishing companies that ignore basic rules of book marketing and leave hundreds of thousands of dollars on the table.

Just look at the top 100 books on Amazon. Do they all come in three different formats? They don't, and that's only one of the numerous things they are missing out on. By implementing the 10 strategies I mentioned above, you should be able to quickly grow your income, your influence, and your brand as an Amazon author.

Book-Writing Myths

There are quite a few myths about writing your own book that I've heard people talk about. In this section, we will dispel all of those myths, including that you need a fancy publisher, your book takes years to write, or you need to be an Olympic gold medalist or accomplished rocket scientist to write a book.

Myth #1: You Need a Fancy Publisher

The traditional publishing industry has been changing rapidly since the introduction of Amazon's Kindle KDP publishing platform. In the old days, if you wanted to write a book, you would have to submit your manuscript to 100 different publishers and get rejected by nearly every single one.

If somehow you were lucky enough to get your book published, the process would often take years to get into bookstores or other book outlets, and then if your book didn't sell well in the first couple of months, it would be taken off of the shelves.

Not only that, but most authors who are signed to traditional publishing deals earn as little as 7% of the profit from their book. Fortunately, with Amazon you have the option to make 35-70%, depending on what price you set your book at.

Amazon has changed the game and made it possible for independent self-publishers like yourself to not only compete on the same level as authors from big-name publishing companies, but to absolutely crush them with good writing and the right marketing.

We will go over that part later in this guide. You can hire professional writers who will edit your book, graphic designers, and book formatters for affordable prices who will have your book looking the same as any other bestselling book. Then, if you are a smart marketer, you can get your book to rank higher than big-name authors and books.

Myth #2: It Takes Years to Write a Book

When people think about writing a book, they

often feel they need to spend three years locked away in their writing cave. Keep in mind that a large percentage of people who buy books don't even read them, and there are things called short stories. Whether your book is non-fiction or fiction, you can write as little as 5,000 or 10,000 words, even though I would recommend 10,000 words as a minimum.

As long as you get your message across, there is no requirement that your book has to be a 12-hour read or anything crazy like that. I know many authors who publish a book a month on something they are passionate about.

If you write just 500 words a day over the course of a month, that is 15,000 words – more than enough words for a book or at least a beginner's guide to your topic.

Writing an outline is the key to being able to write a significant number of words per day. When I have a good outline based on other outlines of similar books and my own experiences, I can easily write 3,000 words per day, which is over one million words per year if I did that every day.

One year of focused writing on different subjects could set you up for life with the passive income, notoriety, and opportunities you will get from that. In fact, one of my bestselling books, *21 Ways to Find Off-Market Real Estate*, took me about a week to write, but it offers a ton of value and combines personal stories and practical tips, so it has become very popular.

Myth #3: You Need to Be a Nobel Prize Winner to Write a Book

Authors come in all shapes and sizes. Don't ever think that you need to have won a gold medal or traveled to the moon to write a book. If you have a passion and are knowledgeable about it, then you can write a book about it. Many times, writing a beginner's guide to whatever subject you want can be a great start to your writing career.

A book is just a much longer and better version of a blog. Anyone can write a blog, and anyone can write a book. I was talking to my friend the other day about writing a book. She didn't know what to write about. She loves cats, and I told her she could write a book about getting her first cat, or how to adopt a cat or any number of cat-related topics. That is just an example, but everyone has that one thing they are passionate about and would love to write about.

Plenty of authors don't even know their subject that well and publish it under a pen name. If you are too timid to publish a book under your name, then use a pen name and publish a few books to get the process down before you release one in your own name.

Some Amazon publishers even hire ghostwriters to write about a subject they are interested in and then publish and optimize the book themselves. On Upwork and other ghostwriting sites, you can pay a ghostwriter around $500 to publish a 10,000-word guide on any topic you want. You just have to give them the outline.

Myth #4: You Don't Know What to Write About

If you are an author struggling with what to write about, here are a few strategies. Get a blank sheet of paper and start writing down topics you think you could write about. To assist with those ideas, you should browse all the top-selling books on Amazon in your subject area of interest and other subjects. You should start to get some ideas of similar books you could write.

It's good to get at least five to 10 ideas so that you can eventually narrow down and choose the best one. Another thought, no matter what business or industry you are in, is to write a guide called *First Time ...* or *Beginner's Guide to ...*, where you can go over all the basic questions and services that a first-time buyer of your product or service may have. The idea is that you want to find topics within your niche that are already selling.

If you write a book that is too specific, nobody will buy it, so follow the proven sellers by coming up with ideas based on already bestselling books.

For example, *The 7 Habits of Highly Effective People* has been a bestseller for decades. If you are a chiropractor and you want to teach other chiropractors, maybe you could write a book called *The 7 Habits of Successful Chiropractors* or something similar. There are countless ways to package information and get it professionally produced.

Myth #5: Your Book Needs to Be Perfect

When I published my first book, I could not afford to have it edited. I gave my friend $50 to go through it and tell me about any mistakes, but that was it. I still published it and started making several hundred dollars per month with mostly good reviews. Too many people think a book has to be completely perfect before you publish.

The great thing about Amazon is that it's very flexible and easy to fix any mistakes you might see. While I don't recommend publishing without an editor, don't be afraid to take action and put it out there.

I can guarantee you, once it's live on Amazon or other distributors, you will make sure you fix any glaring errors or omissions. The second book you publish will be a much easier and smooth process.

Common Book-Writing Mistakes

When you're a self-publishing author, there are several mistakes that can just kill your sales. These are simple things that can be fixed inexpensively and easily, yet many authors don't do that.

Some of this may sound familiar, but I need to emphasize various points about self-publishing so you can build your income and brand. From having published 15 books, these are the top mistakes I would avoid.

1. Pricing Your Book Too High

The first mistake that happens all too often is wrong pricing. Many first-time authors think their book is special just because it's theirs, and they may try to charge a premium price like $15.99. Unless you are Tim Ferris or already have a massive following, you are going to get significantly more sales at a low price.

I always recommend keeping your book price as low as possible when you are getting started ($.99 or $2.99) and only raising your price once you have good reviews and some traction. Since it is so easy to change your price, you can and should always experiment with different price points to see the result on sales, but in most cases, you should start as low as possible.

2. Not Spending Time On Their Cover Or Title

We've gone over the importance of strategically coming up with your cover and title in a previous section, but I just wanted to reiterate how important it is. In fact, for one of my recent books, I spent $1,000 just for a cover design. You don't need to spend that much but make sure your cover and title are highly optimized.

3. Not Writing A Book Description

You need to spend time optimizing your book description. Instead of just writing a sentence or two, you should use HTML formatting, SEO and keywords, and base your description on other best selling authors. In fact, if you want to, just use my book descriptions as a framework for your own.

4. Writing Only 1 Book

If you want to make a full-time income as an author as I do, then you need to write a series of books. The great thing about a series is that no matter what topic you are passionate about, there is an opportunity to create a series and build your brand.

Think of JK Rowling, Chuck Palahniuk, James Patterson, Robert Kiyosaki, and others. Some of these authors have 10, 20, or even over 30 different books to their name. You should try to build an audience of raving fans for your books and offer them more and more products and books. Amazon does a great job of cross-promoting your different books before customers reach the checkout page.

5. Not Optimizing The Author Profile

Another huge mistake authors make is that they don't optimize their Amazon author profile.

Amazon has a ton of SEO potential, so if you fill out your profile correctly, anybody searching you or your name will see your Amazon author profile first.

The Amazon author profile is a great place to add your picture, a mini-biography, a list of your available books, as well as other information like videos, links to your social media, blogs, and more.

If you browse around different authors, even famous ones, you can see how many authors are missing out on this key strategy. To fill yours out correctly, make sure you fill out the profile completely with a picture, mini-biography, any videos you have, and of course all of your books. You can also feel free to model my Amazon Author Profile.

6. Not Researching The Market

If you publish a book, you must make sure there is a market for it. Amazon is too competitive to not do some strategic research to see what types of books are selling. Look in your niche for the bestselling books and come up with ideas for your book based on those.

7. Getting Discouraged

Once you publish your book, you may have visions of being on TV and becoming a millionaire. While that certainly could happen, more than likely you will have to build your brand over time.

Keep publishing, keep marketing, and set realistic goals. When I was getting started, I was thrilled when I made my first $100 per month. To get through the "suck phase," you have to put out a lot of content and optimize the content so that some of it can take off and start making recurring income.

8. Not Editing Your Book

We've covered this, but I still see author's make this mistake all the time. Get your book professionally edited with one of the aforementioned services.

9. Not Formatting Your Book

We've also talked about this, but if you want your

book to look great then make sure to use a professional book formatting expert. The last thing you want to do is just throw a book up on Amazon and hope it sells.

10. Not Building An Email List

If you want to be a successful author, your goal should be to build a large email list. Nearly every successful author I know has told me that this was their #1 regret when getting started. They all wished they had built their list earlier.

Resources For Authors

———✦———

The self-publishing industry is a rapidly evolving business and on my website www.jeff-leighton.com I keep track of all the best resources for authors like yourself. I could list them here however they might change over the course of a few months or years so I decided it was best to keep an updated list on my aforementioned website. You can access this list for free of vendors that I personally use and recommend.

This resource list includes the following:

- Book Editors
- Cover Designers
- Book Formatting Professionals
- Free Tools For Self-Publishers
- Paid Tools For Self-Publishers
- Recommended Authors To Follow
- Recommended Videos On The Self-Publishing Business

- Book Distribution Companies To Utilize In Addition To Amazon
- Productivity Tools
- Author Communities And Mastermind Groups
- Author Events
- The Best Survey Companies For Getting Feedback On Your Work
- Organization Tools
- And much, much more...

Now It's Time to Publish Your Book

At first glance, writing a book can seem like an overwhelming task that most people would think requires years and years, only to have your book rejected by a publishing company. Fortunately, the book industry has changed.

I have provided step-by-step instructions on how to publish your own book based on your interests, expertise, or topic. Not only that but in most scenarios, you can even do better than if a large publishing company had published your book.

This guide contains everything you need to know to successfully publish your book and start making a passive income today.

The steps in this book are the exact steps I took to publish numerous Amazon bestsellers, so make sure you reference different sections if you have any questions.

If you are looking for additional training on self-publishing successfully, then I would recommend you check out the book-publishing programs on my website.

I invested in countless books and self-publishing courses before writing my books, and in my programs, I include only the best of the best material to help you become a successful author.

If you are serious about becoming an author and want to take your publishing to the next level, then I highly recommend checking it out.

Thanks for reading, and I wish you a ton of future success with your book!

Jeff Leighton

PS If you enjoyed this book and received a lot of value from it, I would appreciate it if you left a helpful review on Amazon. Thanks!

About The Author

Jeff Leighton is a real estate investor and bestselling Amazon Author. He has studied many of the top-selling authors and has self-published over 15 books including several Amazon bestsellers. He is passionate about marketing and helping entrepreneurs successfully launch their book and take their business to the next level.

Want More Training?

Go to www.jeff-leighton.com for helpful videos, free resources, downloads, additional mentoring, online programs, and much, much more.

Other Books By The Author

Available on Amazon

Follow Jeff Leighton

Instagram.com/J_Late12
YouTube.com/JeffLeighton1
Facebook.com/JeffLeighton5